ALEXANDRE TANSMAN
VISIT TO ISRAEL

Suite for Piano

	PAGE	
Notturno	1	*Notturno*
The Kibbutz	2	*Le Kibboutz*
The Ruins of Capernaum	4	*Les ruines de Kaphernaoum*
The Sources of the River Jordan	5	*Les sources du Jourdain*
The Holy City	6	*La ville sainte*
The Desert of Negev	8	*Le désert du Néguev*
The Mosque of Saint Jean d'Acre	9	*La mosquee de Saint Jean d'Acre*
The Lake of Tiberias	11	*Le lac de Tibériade*
Yemenite Cradle Song	12	*Chant a berger Yéménite*
Popular Dance	14	*Danse populaire*

ISBN 978-1-4803-9308-0

EDWARD B. MARKS MUSIC COMPANY

EXCLUSIVELY DISTRIBUTED BY

HAL•LEONARD® CORPORATION

7777 W. BLUEMOUND RD. P.O. BOX 13819 MILWAUKEE, WI 53213

www.ebmarks.com
www.halleonard.com

VISIT TO ISRAEL
(DIX FEUILLETS DE VOYAGE)

SUITE FOR PIANO

Alexandre TANSMAN

to Elfi and Wolfgang Schocken

1. NOTTURNO
(The Mysterious City of Tz'fat)

1. NOTTURNO
(La Mystérieuse Cité de Sefad)

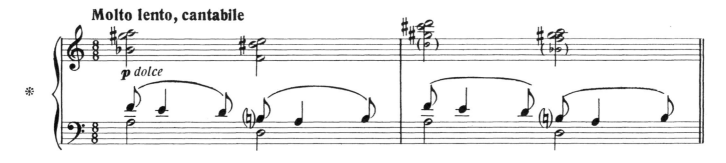

✻ *Les accidents sont marqués séparément pour chaque main.*
The Accidentals are marked separately for each hand.

to Dr. Y. Spira

2. THE KIBBUTZ

2. LE KIBBOUTZ

to Denise and François Nérault

3. THE RUINS OF CAPERNAUM

3. LES RUINES DE KAPHERNAOUM

Lento malinconico

to Dr. and Mrs. Pickart

4. THE SOURCES OF THE RIVER JORDAN   4. LES SOURCES DU JOURDAIN

to Gaby and Charles Bruck

5. THE HOLY CITY

(The Seven-armed Candelabra)

5. LA VILLE SAINTE

(Le Chandelier à Sept Branches)

Allegro moderato

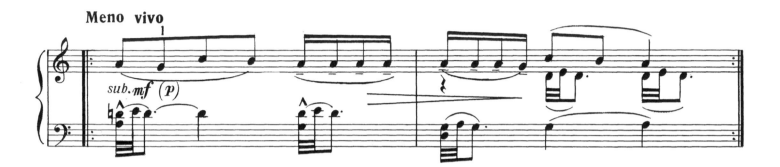

to Mrs. Fernand Halphen

6. THE DESERT OF NEGEV

6. LE DÉSERT DU NÉGUEV

Lento

sempre **pp** *tranquillo*

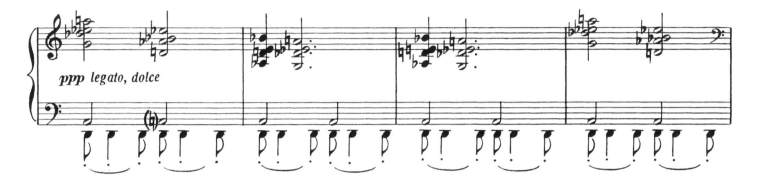

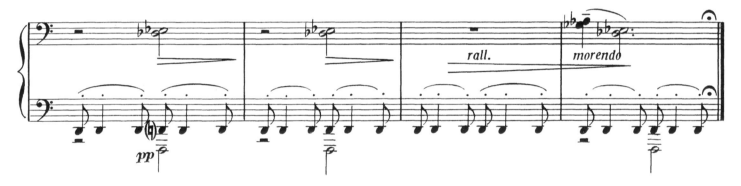

to Mr. and Mrs. Vladimir Jankélévitch

7. THE MOSQUE OF SAINT JEAN D'ACRE   7. LA MOSQUÉE DE SAINT JEAN D'ACRE

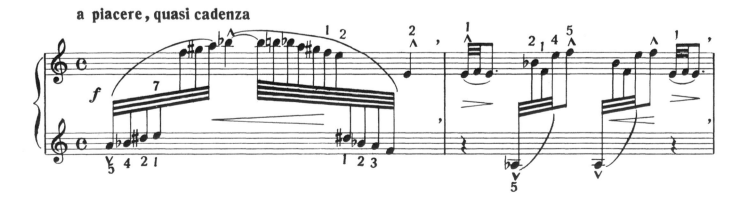

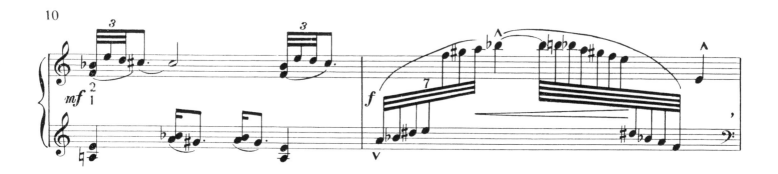

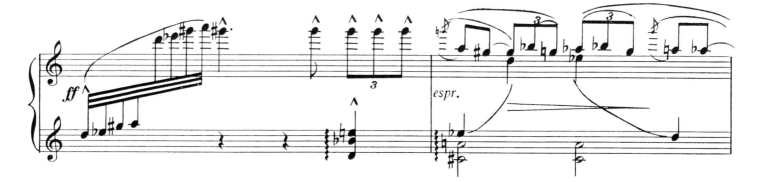

to Pierre Capdevielle

8. THE LAKE OF TIBERIAS   8. LE LAC DE TIBÉRIADE

Moderato

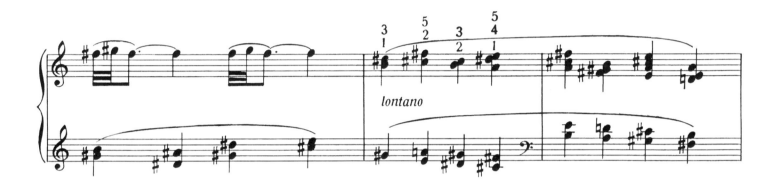

to Suzanne and Pierre - Michel Le Conte

9. YEMENITE CRADLE SONG

9. CHANT A BERCER YÉMÉNITE

Lento cantabile

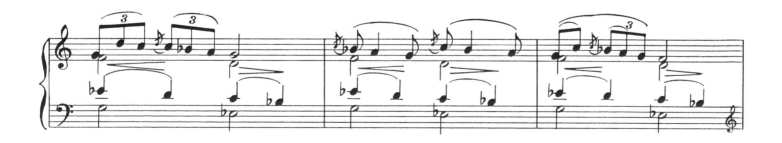

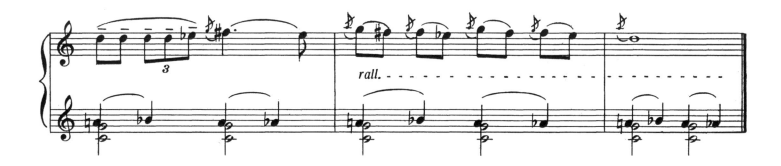

to Anna and Tino Ambrosetti

10. POPULAR DANCE
(Hora)

10. DANSE POPULAIRE
(Hora)

sempre animando

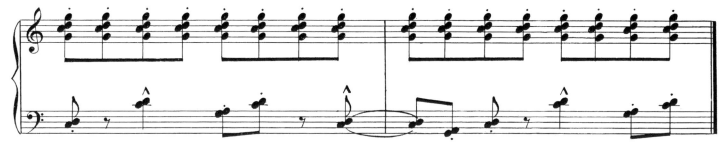

Paris X- X I -1958